# Through My Eyes

Deb —

Thankyou for all of your
support and love over the years.
I cherish our friendship more than
you know. Thankyou for
believing in me.
I love you.
A. Piper Childs

# A LETTER TO A RAPIST

## Through My
## Eyes

# PYPER CHILDS

| Library of Congress Control Number: | | 2010919408 |
| --- | --- | --- |
| ISBN: | Hardcover | 978-1-4535-8203-9 |
| | Softcover | 978-1-4535-8202-2 |
| | Ebook | 978-1-4535-8204-6 |

This book was printed in the United States of America.

**To order additional copies of this book, contact:**
Xlibris Corporation
1-888-795-4274
www.Xlibris.com
Orders@Xlibris.com
86395

# Contents

All conversations and events in this book are as I perceived them through my eyes. However, in order to protect those in this book, all names have been changed, including mine.

To all the men, women, and children who have and have not survived any act of violence. God bless you.

A special thanks to my family, friends, and Kelly for all of your support, trust, and love. Without you, I would not have come so far, so fast. Thank you.

I also want to thank Brooke and Xlibris Corporation for your help in completing this part of my healing and journey.

## *Prologue*

*H*ave you ever been inspired or felt like you needed a change? Has something ever consumed your every thought, and the only way to push it out of your mind is to do something about it? Have you ever wanted to be heard? I have, and that is why I have written what you are about to read.

I spent most of my childhood trying to associate with the "in" crowd, only to find out once I was in, I wanted to be out. I found myself picking and choosing who my friends were based on what the group saw as *cool* instead of associating myself with healthy people and true friends. Yet these friends never called me when I was home for college breaks, they rarely included me on the group e-mail chains, and I was not in their high school yearbook collage. So why was I trying so hard to be friends with people who did not put the same effort into our friendship that I did?

It is a question I ask myself to this day. My closest friend, who will be my maid of honor at my wedding, whenever that may be, stood by me while I attempted to find myself. It was not until about five years ago that I decided to make a difference and stand up for what I believe and know to be right. I am finally at peace with who I am and I do not care if those *cool friends* do not call me. I am perfectly content knowing that I have a handful of lifetime friends and a great family who will stand by me through thick and thin. Granted, it took me many years and a traumatic event to clarify all of this.

Some people experience trauma and shut out everyone who cares and loves them. Some prefer to get out frustrations, fears, and anxiety internally and take it upon themselves to exercise, listen to music, or take a drive. Then there are the many who decide to cope in unhealthy ways; through drinking, drugs, violence, self-mutilation, or perhaps suicide. Even though all situations of trauma are different, the outcome is often very similar. People who cope with trauma often find themselves reliving the trauma, in anguish, or often suppressing the memories of the experience to never have to think about it again. These people continue their destructive behavior and often end up lost.

When my trauma happened, I felt all of those things and more. I dealt with the coping, memory, fear, distrust, feeling of loss, along with the mental, emotional, and physical aspects of trauma and the process of healing.

Let me clarify. I am not a therapist, doctor, or psychologist. I am definitely not a professional writer. You will not get the detailed descriptions, powerful words, or anything that a well crafted writer can create. What you will get is the truth. You will get the truth in the realest way. Because I am not a professional writer, you will read this story as I am no different than your child, sibling, friend, or lover. I am a typical young adult. I just happen to have a story to tell.

One day I sat down and started writing a letter to my best friend who raped me. Before I knew it, I had expressed all of my feelings in over thirty pages. I am not sure if I ever planned on sending it to him; for me, it was more of a healing piece than anything else. As I wrote page after page, I began to discover feelings and issues that I did not even realize were present until I started writing. This letter goes through my life, tested friendships, personal growth, and my healing through this traumatic experience.

I am not sharing my story to become famous, to be interviewed, or to go on book tours. I am no different than any of the other billions of survivors of violence. I just chose to write about it. I hope it helps the issue become a reality. Acts of violence should not be associated with feelings of shame and embarrassment. They are real and more common than people like to admit.

My goal is threefold. First, I would like the reader to come out learning at least one thing, no matter what that thing may be. Second, by reading this book and talking about this book, we together are raising awareness. Lastly, my most important goal is to prevent at least one person from having to become a survivor of or performing an act of violence.

After five years of journaling, meeting with a counselor, and speaking twice at my alma mater, there is still more I can do. I can write a book. So here I am, sharing my story in graphic detail. Thank you for taking the time to make a difference.

## Step 1

## Remember Me?

ear Jason,

Where do I even begin? It has been over five years. The emotions that I have felt over the past five years are some that I have never felt in the past twenty-six. There is so much that I wish I could say. But the truth is, I have said it, you either didn't listen or didn't believe me.

Sometimes I wonder if we sat down and went over that night how different our sides would be. I already know where some of our friends stand. It makes me sick to my stomach that some of our mutual friends think the entire thing was blown out of proportion, exaggerated, or unnecessary. Unnecessary? Absolutely. It never should have happened. But blown out of proportion and exaggerated? Absolutely not.

If it was something to be brushed under the rug, I wouldn't still be struggling and healing. If it didn't happen, I wouldn't have anything to heal from. Nobody would ever wish this pain on anyone, and I promise you, no one could ever make it up. It is suffocating, exhausting, traumatizing, terrifying, demoralizing, depressing, frustrating, and every other feeling that ends in "ing" - including fucking annoying.

I find myself often wondering if you have learned anything, if you remember that summer and that night? If you remember the friendship we had developed the previous five years and how it was all thrown to the curb in one night . . . one hour. Would you do it again? Do you think it was a big deal? Does it bother you that we haven't spoken in years? Or, that the few times we have seen each other that I just want to punch you in the face? How do you believe you have the right to be in my presence? How do you have the gall to associate yourself with people who know what happened? And why do those people continue to associate with you?

I wonder if I ever cross your mind nearly as much as you cross mine. Unfortunately, I think about you every day, sometimes twenty times a day. Thoughts about that night, thoughts about what you have done since, if you have learned anything, if you have done it again, if there were women before me - how do you look at yourself in the mirror?

Every time I watch a violent movie, watch the news, or talk to friends who are survivors of violence or abuse, I get a rush of emotions. It can be something as little as hearing the McDonalds' "I'm lovin'it" jingle.

Things that used to bring so much joy to my life now bring doubt, distrust, concern, and high sensitivity. I'm always on alert, always watching my back, and uncomfortable around new males in my life. I only give someone new about thirty seconds before I have a read on them and trust them or not. One negative feel and that is it - they lost their chance. I fear everyday that this will happen again, and I often find myself living in fear of something happening, instead of enjoying the moment and being grateful for what I do have and for how far I have come since that disturbing night.

I won't go to the bathroom or walk to my car alone. There are nights I don't feel like going out because I simply have a gut feeling that I shouldn't. I cannot recall a time in the past five years that I have gone to a male's house alone without knowing it is safe or until I know that I am safe with him. That inner voice that I ignored so much that night is something that I have never, and will never ignore again.

For some reason, perhaps because of pictures that I come across or stories that I hear, I can just imagine that you pretend like that night never happened. Thanks to the joys of Facebook® I came across your profile picture and I started crying. I went to write a birthday message on our friend from the beach Cailey's Facebook® Wall, and a birthday wish from you was her last post. Your picture showed you with your arms open, and you had this cocky smirk on your face. You looked so proud. It made me sick to my stomach.

I could hear your words; they were so familiar even though I hadn't spoken to you in years. They seemed so sincere and loving, yet I know you. I know how conniving, manipulating, and fake you are. Seeing that message was the straw that broke the camel's back for me to write this letter.

I cannot watch or hear about you hurting another person. I cannot watch you suck the life out of someone else. I cannot hear one more person tell me how much they do not trust you. I cannot tolerate another one of our friends bitching to me about you. I don't care about you! I don't want you in my life. Why are you still around? I hate that we are in the same group. I hate that we have the same friends. I hate what happened that night. I hate how I am no longer innocent. I hate that you still have control over me. I hate that I have to see you, and I hate that I now have something that every relationship in the future should know about.

Have you learned anything, or do you think I'm still just making up all of this? Do I ever cross your mind? Do you feel any remorse or guilt? Do you know that what happened that night was wrong? When are you going to take responsibility for your actions instead of just floating along like you are so innocent? I know the truth. I know who you are deep down. I will never forget it. I can't forget. And even though we haven't spoken in over five years, you still control me. The only difference is this time you aren't controlling my body; you are indirectly controlling my mind and actions. And the only way I know how to minimize it is to do what I have been doing - focusing on taking care of myself.

## Step 2

## The Good Days

*I* still remember the first time we met. We were seventeen. It was at the First Aid / CPR class at the Yacht Club that all sailing instructors had to take before the new summer season. It was my second summer instructing. We were all there, and then there was you. You were wearing a winter beanie on your head; and I remember thinking *cute, but what is he all about?* You were new, and usually it was pretty hard to break the border to get into our group. We had all been best friends since we were thirteen. Even during the school year, we would talk frequently and spend every day and night of the summer working and partying together. I thought to myself that there was no chance you were going to ruin what we had. Interesting irony don't you think?

I watched boyfriends and girlfriends be shunned from the group, and fellow instructors or coworkers try to hang out, and so many failed.

Not because we weren't welcoming, but because we had so many inside jokes, memories, stories, and a bond that was untouchable. However, this time was different. It was because our mutual friend Mark was giving you a chance, I figured you must be okay. Surprisingly, you seemed to fit in more than hurt us. You were funny, charming, and witty. Do you remember that we were partners for the CPR dummy and we laughed the entire two hours and the teacher of the class was so angry at the five of us? He made us do push ups and sit ups if we misbehaved. I think we were doing them all night!

After the class, we went our own ways; I didn't know what Yacht Club you were going to be coaching, and I really didn't know where you had come from or anything about you. I still didn't know how you and Mark knew one another or how I had never met you before. I had been in the group and I had never laid eyes on you. It wasn't until a few months later when summer came that I got my answers.

## Step 3

## You Were My Rock

It was that summer of 2000 when it all began. We had just finished our sophomore year in high school. Looking back, we were so young. Do you remember that we hit it off immediately? I can remember you joining the group, and we went from four to five. There was an attraction between the two of us. We would innocently flirt, talk almost every night, and throw back and forth sexual innuendos. It was like you were my wingman. We would sit next to each other, defend one another, and laugh with each other. I still remember that night we jumped the border of the highway to make it to the ice cream place before it closed. While on the water, as we coached, we would drive past each other and wave, wink, or smirk. I remember loving going to regattas to coach because the five of us would have the best time together. It was fun, and it was innocent.

Remember all the nights we would go to the beach and watch fireworks? Or, go to the boardwalk to get ice cream and laugh at all the people who looked like they dressed in the dark? We did everything together. We were one of those close-knit groups that if you called one person, it was assumed everyone else was invited, no questions asked. It was incredible and a bond like nothing I had ever known before.

It was during our senior year of high school that I truly appreciated our friendship. It was the year of my Dad's heart attack. You were there for me all night while I cried and was terrified I'd lose him. I didn't know what do to, but you were there and brought me stability and peace. You seemed to always have the right things to say, and my trust in you continued to grow.

Emergency triple bypass open-heart surgery. I can remember the day like it was yesterday. I was coming back from lunch, and my teacher was waiting for me at the entrance. I remember thinking it was a bit strange, but I was happy to see her. She took me to the principal's office to inform me of the news. The entire experience was surreal. I can remember being taken to the hospital and waiting for the surgery to finish. It was supposed to be a six-hour surgery, and the only thing we could do was wait. I have memories of calling loved ones and breaking the news. I remember leaning on you. Needing you.

I can remember when the doctor came out and slowly walked over with no expression and no emotion. And my Mom, Brother, and I were on the brink of a meltdown. I recall the smell of the antiseptic and bleach. The image of seeing my Dad for the first time in the ICU after he fought his out-of-body experience and came back to us, is imprinted in my brain.

I went to the hospital two or three times a day for the next few weeks. The vision of seeing someone who I felt was so strong, unbreakable, and invincible in his weakest state was a scene I will never forget. A few weeks later he was released from the hospital and we would go on walks together; and then one day he made it to my soccer game. I'll never forget how proud I was that he was not only at my game, but he was alive.

I remember the pain, confusion, frustration, and anger I had at myself. How did I almost lose my Dad? I wanted to make up for all the lost years and take back all the fights. And I reminisce it was you who supported me and helped me realize that it was a blessing that he was alive and that it was the future I could focus on.

# Step 4

## Survivors

*I* was at my friend's house when I got a phone call from my Mom telling me to get home immediately. I was driving up my street as the ambulance raced passed me. I didn't know what had happened. I was expecting the worst. I walked in the door and my Mom was barely holding it together, and she had always been the strongest woman I have ever known. I think I had seen her cry a handful of times in my life, and one of those times was six weeks prior when Dad had the heart attack. My Mom and I went to the hospital, and she informed me that she believed Dad had a stroke. When we got to the hospital, we raced to the emergency room and waited to be brought back to Dad. That familiar smell of antiseptic and bleach radiated through me. I held back tears as we rushed down the sterile hallway. Do you remember any of this?

He was paralyzed down his right side and couldn't speak. Doctor after doctor kept arriving trying to analyze him, and he was lying in a hospital bed with the most dazed look I had ever seen. It was like he was talking to us but couldn't understand why we weren't responding. But we were the ones talking to him without getting an answer.

There was a checklist from the doctors. The amount of time since the heart attack, the last time he had eaten, at least three hours since the stroke, and more. Once again God was on his side and everything was in place. Dad qualified for what some call "the miracle drug," and what doctors call T-pa. The goal of T-pa is to reverse a stroke. I'm not sure how it does it, but it does. If nothing else it gave Dad a chance.

About an hour passed and more doctors came in and the smell of that hospital seemed to permeate right through me. A doctor handed Dad a pen and tried to get him to say *pen*. I could see his eyes focus and his mouth quiver, but no words were coming out. He kept looking at the pen and then looking at Mom and me, not understanding why the doctor was still holding the pen in front of him. In his mind he had clearly stated that it was a pen; however, no words came out. He grew frustrated as more doctors came in.

The next doctor asked him to say his name; once again no words, just frustration. He kept trying and trying, and finally he squealed out, "Billy!" It was a blessing he spoke, but Mom's face said it all. She was terrified that he had reverted back to his childhood and that when he would recover from the stroke, his body would be fifty, but his mind would be five.

It wasn't until about the tenth doctor that God returned. The doctor walked in, and Dad put out his right hand to shake the doctor's hand. I remember everyone continued to look at the monitors and write scribble on their clipboards and continued to try to get him to talk. It felt like time elapsed painfully slow as I watched from the outside in shock that not a single doctor realized that my Dad, who was paralyzed for hours on his right side, just lifted his right hand to shake a doctor's hand.

Maybe the trauma with my Dad was all meant to prepare me for the trauma you caused me. My Dad was a survivor and so am I.

Our lives continued, and Dad continued therapy as he slowly regained his ability to speak and walk. There isn't a day that goes by that I do not think it is a blessing that he is alive. And I'm pretty sure there wasn't a day while he was in the hospital that we didn't talk and you didn't genuinely ask how he was doing and how I was doing. You were there for me.

Dad just had his eighth anniversary this past year of his heart attack and stroke. It took me until about four years ago to accept what had happened, that it was out of my control and that I can be at peace knowing that I love my Dad no matter what the circumstance. It is an unconditional love. Ironically, it has taken me five years to accept what had happened between you and me, that it was out of my control and that I can be at peace knowing that I love myself no matter what the circumstance. Can you say the same?

## *Step 5*

## *Foreshadow*

*I*n between everything that was going on at home, school, and sports, I still attempted to live a normal childhood and adolescence. I looked forward to coming down to the beach to see you and everyone else because it made me happy and I felt safe. I knew the struggles from the previous year would temporarily vanish and I would be able to open up and let myself have fun. Things had been so intense and serious since Dad was sick that it was the summers I looked forward to the most.

The summers seemed to go faster and faster each year. However, as close as we would get during the summers, it was during the school year we really got to know each other. It was all the late phone calls each night and the chats on Instant Messenger. I recall anxiously awaiting holiday breaks so we could all meet up at Mark's house at the beach. Those winter reunions were always the best. We would catch up on the fall, play drinking games, laugh, and continue our bond. It's funny how now I always question going to the beach over the holidays. Yet another joy you have stripped from me.

In 2002, we were both at college and found ourselves in relationships. I remember continuing to speak with you often, sharing stories about our ups and downs of college relationships, and when the time would come that we would all meet.

It was that next summer that we had our first fling in the time we had known each other. That attraction had always been there, but for some reason, it was that night on the beach that changed it all. I made the choice to cheat on Todd to be with you. I remember the first kiss and my hesitation. Yet you were persistent, so I let my guard down and went with it. Granted we didn't sleep together, but the damage was already done. It wasn't until the next morning I remember feeling terrible. I wish I realized that omen. With you was the one and only time I had ever cheated. It's almost comical how you have taught me so many life lessons, through so many negative experiences.

It wasn't until the summer of 2005 when we were both going into our senior year of college that things were altered once again. For the first time we were both single. We were inseparable and had not hooked up since the night on the beach a few years prior. To me, your friendship was much more important than the sexual relationship we once had.

I still have so many pictures from that summer that I occasionally come across. Pictures of hugs, laughter, smiles, and genuine happiness filter through my photo albums. It was the summer we took Mark's boat to the flats and played in the water all day. We were playing in tubes, wake boarding, jet skiing, and drinking. We stayed on the water until dinner and then went to eat by boat. Do you have a copy of the picture of me in the tube in my blue bikini and you were standing behind me hugging me? I came across it the other day and shook my head at how close we once were.

I never could have known how the dynamics would change; that I would be writing this letter, with no group chemistry and no group at all.

# Step 6

## The Beginning of the End

That one night ruined everything. Do you remember it as vividly as I do? We were all hanging out at Mark's house getting ready to do our normal pregame routine before we hit the bars. It was laid back like usual; card games, beer pong, and kings. The TV was on in the background, although no one was watching. Artists like Matis Yahu, MXPX, and Taking Back Sunday were blaring; some of us were out at the tiki bar; and we were all casually drinking while getting ready to head out to the bars.

After everyone was ready, we headed out. The usual crowd was there, and we got our free drinks from the bartender and started taking shots. We danced upstairs like idiots, but we were all having a blast. We stayed until two in the morning, and we then went back to Mark's. We all stayed up longer, playing more cards and beer pong until we all started to crash. At some point I fell asleep on the couch. I was exhausted, figuring I'd get drawn on or laughed at in the morning because I passed out early like usual. The rest of the group was still playing cards and drinking, but I could not hold my head up. I remember randomly waking up and hearing the music get turned down as everyone else was either heading home or to bed. It was probably around four in the morning.

I guess you had noticed that I was passed out. I assume, being my best friend, that you felt it would be best for me to go to sleep in a bed. The thing was, it wasn't atypical and no one blinked an eye when they saw you guide me out of the room, through the hallway, and into the queen bedroom. You were a trusted friend. As I came to consciousness, I asked you what was going on. You reminded me that I had been passed out on the couch and you were trying to get me to go to bed so I could have a good night sleep. I don't know what your definition of a good night sleep was, but if I was already passed out on the couch, I probably wouldn't have noticed the difference between a couch and a bed. Regardless, I went with you and felt safe. After all, we had shared a bed in the past, why would that night be any different?

I was in that pink dress that I still wear today for some reason and love, even though every time I wear it I remember that night. Perhaps I wear it because in some strange way it makes what you did to me real. It reminds me how far I have come since that night and how much stronger I am each time I wear it compared to the last.

I couldn't get the zipper undone. I stumbled over to you, using the wall and bed to stabilize myself, laughing as I realized how drunk I really was. I remember turning my back to you innocently asking for you to unzip the back of my dress. I considered you my closest friend, I never even thought twice about the task.

As I continued to get ready for bed, in my underwear searching for a pair of Mark's shorts to wear, we began to fool around for the first time since that one time on the beach. It was passionate and powerful. The years of waiting had brought intensity to the night that I had never experienced. However, apparently, what I was imagining was different than what you were thinking.

## *Step 7*

## *The Rape*

My innocent and flirtatious make out had turned into you on top of me and inside of me. It took a few minutes to really absorb how quickly things occurred and truly had gotten out of my control. Once the pieces started falling into place, I pushed my arms on your shoulders to push you off of me. I remember closing my eyes for a minute, to take a second to think about what was going on. You saw my hesitation and responded with, "What's wrong?"

In trying to process everything since I had already been blacked out, I said, "Wait, give me a second, I don't think this is a good idea." It was then that you stated something along the lines of, "It's fine, this is nothing, c'mon."

As I had in the past, I put my trust in you, my best friend, and put my arms down as you continued to thrust inside of me. My head was spinning and I was not in it at all. I was lying there, trying to process everything as thoughts were racing through my mind like, *Wait, I'm not on the pill. You're not using a condom and I don't want to be doing this. Should I stop this? This can't really be happening right now! I don't like this.*

Finally, after what felt like eternity, I stated, "C'mon, this is a bad idea, Jason, I'm not on the pill, and we don't have a condom." At this point, you pulled out your penis and tried to console me by saying, "Don't worry about it. Pre-cum doesn't do anything. You're fine, stop stressing." Without letting me respond, you continued to penetrate me. Immediately I said, "Jason, seriously c'mon this isn't fun for me." Is it coming back to you now? Does it seem right as you read it through my eyes?

The night took a quick turn for the worse. Instead of listening, you told me to roll over so you could continue your wrong act. I remember hesitating and telling you that I didn't want to roll over. I didn't know if you were going to sodomize me or just continue to have sex with me. My mind continued to try to take it all in; it was happening so fast. I couldn't process anything, and before I knew it, you were adjusting your weight so I had the space to roll over as you moved me with your hands.

I couldn't see your face, the room was pitch black, I felt the tears in my eyes building, my body got tense, and I didn't know what else to do. I felt like I wasn't there, as if my mind went somewhere else. I didn't want to be there; it had gone too far, and you weren't listening to me. Why didn't you listen? You ruined everything we had built.

It was after about two thrusts when I finally got the strength and rolled over, and pushed you off of me. I remember you jumped right up, seeing the tears in my eyes. The room was silent, it was like time had stopped, and you could only hear the river and crickets outside. I watched you as you took a step back. It was like a light bulb went on as I watched your silhouette react as you realized what had transpired. You quickly gathered your pants and left. You left me by myself - in a dark room, naked, alone, and scared - thinking about what had happened. And you didn't say a word.

## Step 8

### Alone

You probably didn't realize what happened to me after you left. I began to cry and shake. I no longer felt drunk, but instead confused and violated. How did my best friend just take advantage of me? I began to blame myself and felt that I was not direct enough with you. Could I have done something differently to stop you? Why did you bring me upstairs in the first place? I began to wonder if I had actually said the word "no." Would that have made any difference?

Somehow, with a mind full of thoughts and worry I fell asleep, hoping to wake up from an awful dream. Instead, when I woke up, you were in the bed lying next to me. I don't know at what time you thought you had the right to be back in that room with me. I remember getting up that morning and you tried to talk to me like nothing was wrong. I recall my returned shock and getting out of bed trying to ignore you as I gathered my things in a hurry.

The room was bright from the sunrise, and I could hear the boats starting their day on the river. This was scenery of beauty that should have made me feel peaceful and serene, yet you ruined that for me. Instead, I felt like it was a gloomy rainy day with no hint of sun.

I remember walking downstairs, and Mark was already awake. He smirked at me. To this day I'm not sure if it was because he assumed we hooked up or if you had said something to him, bragging to him that we hooked up. However, nothing about the night was hooking up; it was violent, and it was wrong.

I left Mark's house and went to Kevin's house. Kevin had always been in the group and now that I couldn't trust you or Mark, he was the only one I could confide in. I remember sitting on his front porch quietly, trying to find the words. He could tell something was wrong and started asking me questions about what had happened after he left the late-night activities. Tears started to form in my eyes as I began to tell Kevin what you did to me.

Once I had finished gathering all of my thoughts, I remember looking up at Kevin and seeing his face in disbelief. Unlike you, Kevin listened to me and tried to take it all in. I could see him trying to process how one of his best friends could ever do this to someone. Kevin asked if I would press charges, and I wondered why Kevin would even ask me that.

Kevin's response was, "Pyper, you were raped."

I don't know whether or not I was willing to admit or accept it, but once he said the words I knew it was the truth.

You were my best friend. Why would you do this? You must have noticed that I was uncomfortable. Didn't you realize I was trying to stop you? You kept giving me excuses about why your actions were justified. How could this have happened? You raped me. And Kevin wanted me to report you.

But imagine the rumors, the lawsuits, the he said she said, the pain, the lies. Looking back, that would have all been worth it; and I wonder to this day why I never did report you. I am not sure I even grasped the concept that reporting you was a real option. Perhaps that is why you are receiving this letter. After more than five years of feeling ashamed and wondering if you think about that night or think about me, I had to write to you in order to fully accept and move forward. And maybe, to make you think.

## *Step 9*

# *Betrayal*

*I*'m sure I don't have to remind you, but without a doubt, the group began to struggle. Kevin was having a hard time with what side to support. To me, you raped me. To you, it was a hookup gone bad. And no one else knew, unless you told someone. Kevin was torn. He obviously did not want to feel the pressure or reality of having to choose a side. However, in case you didn't notice, Kevin favored me. At least until a couple of years later when he started to welcome you back into the group. I knew Mark wasn't mature enough to kick you out of his life, but I really thought Kevin would have been different. Life continued, and the rape was pushed to the back of everyone else's minds. Was it pushed to the back of yours?

The rest of that summer was a blur. Nothing seemed to matter. The joy in life was taken away with thoughts of anger, pain, confusion, frustration, violation, and guilt. I remember when I called you the day after the rape. Although I didn't know how much he knew about the previous night, Mark and I were on our way to see a movie. You were willing to talk to me, but you didn't agree with me. Once again you weren't listening to me, to my thoughts, or to my questions. I kept trying to have you hear me, and you just talked over me. It was no different than the previous night, except this time you weren't on top of me and inside of me. I couldn't take it anymore and everything had built up that I yelled, "Jason, you raped me."

"Rape? Come on, what the hell are you talking about? That's an awfully strong word, Pyper."
"Are you serious? You didn't even listen to me. You forced yourself on top of me. What would you call it?"
"No, no, no. It wasn't rape. We were just drunk."

So once again, you didn't listen to me. You didn't believe me. You were too busy defending your own ass to own up to your actions. And the sad thing is you still haven't owned up to it. Will you ever?

On the way to see the movie I updated Mark about what happened the night before and he didn't get it, just like you. No wonder you two are still friends. It wasn't until the middle of the movie when there was a violent rape scene that he grabbed my hand as the tears came running down my face.

That was the first time I realized that night would affect the rest of my life. You made me aware, alert, and highly sensitive to violence. Every movie, every commercial, every joke - I feel the same way. In fact, it is so interesting to me that movies, television shows, and people talk about rape, or joke about rape, like it is not a big deal or it is something funny. I would imagine for me, watching a scene like that is the same for anyone who lost someone on September 11th to watch movies about New York City tragedies.

I respect the directors who use violence in the sense that rape is real, this happens, but I was watching *All about Steve*, with Sandra Bullock, and at one point in the movie something along the lines of "don't rape me" was said as a joke. Similarly, I watched the opening episode of the second season to *Sons of Anarchy* and the main female character gets raped. Every time I see something like that, I relive everything that you did to me. I know rape occurs and educating people is helpful and the right thing to do. However, when it is used for entertainment purposes or humor it is very hard for rape survivors to handle.

When I saw *Slumdog Millionaire*, I felt the same way. There was a scene where a man was torturing young kids. As the scene approached, I immediately got tense and almost walked out of the theater.

I have feelings like this every time I watch a violent movie or happen to be flipping through the television and see *Law and Order: Special Victims Unit*. My Dad watches that show regularly and he does not understand why I refuse to sit down and watch it with him. He gets offended because in his eyes, I do not want to spend time with him. He will say, "We can watch something else," but the damage is already done. The thoughts are already in my head. My Dad fails to understand, but I cannot blame him because he does not know what you did to me. I have never told him about you. The disconnect makes him feel slighted, so he takes it personally, although it really has nothing to do with him; it has everything to do with you.

## Step 10

### Lacking Support

After the night at the movie with Mark, I tried to dodge you every chance I could. The site of you made me cringe. Everyone began to wonder how two best friends became strangers. What did you say to them? How did you explain it to them? I know you tried to talk to me about the night, trying to defend your actions, and justify them; but I couldn't trust you anymore or understand how you saw forcing yourself onto me as right. I knew how I felt, and I knew what had happened to me. I felt disgusted, ashamed, embarrassed, and scared. I did not feel safe in the same room as you. The trust we had developed was gone.

I decided to come home early that summer. I left without closure or anyone really knowing what had happened. When I came home, I had mentioned something to my Mom about the calamity. All I wanted was to have her support. After all, Kevin didn't want to talk about it, Mark didn't believe me, you didn't believe me, who would?

I don't remember how it came up, but she started to ask how my last few weeks at the beach were. She started asking about Mark, Kevin, my childhood girlfriend Kristin, and you. I gathered the courage to say that word one more time, I began to tell her about that night and the rape.

What was my Mom's response? "You know how you get when you're drunk . . . you really need to be more careful." I felt like I was talking to you all over again.

I respect my Mom so much and there are aspects of her that I wish I had, and aspects of her I want to teach my future children. But I want to teach my children that it's okay to not be so traditional too. I love that I expect a guy to open the door, pull out my seat, give me his coat, come up to the door, take out the trash, I do. But it's okay to talk about racial issues, sex, rape, gays, and trauma.

I never said another word to my Mom about you or that night. There are still times out of the blue she will ask if I ever see you. When she does, it is like a knife through my heart. She means no harm, but her casual statement is far from casual to me and it often takes me several hours, and sometimes days to recover. She blamed the rape on alcohol. I love my Mom and she has been incredible to me in every other aspect of my life. She didn't know how to act or what to say. But the truth is you did this, not alcohol.

If you had decided to completely ignore my concerns and insert yourself into me while I was sober, would that have made it right? Or did I choose to be a victim of sexual assault? Did I ask you to rape me? Just because I asked you to unzip my dress or because we started to make out gives you no right or invitation to take advantage of me. It gives you no right to not listen to me, or to convince me, or to rape me. You don't want to admit it was rape? Fine, it still was sexual assault. Does that make you feel better?

My Mom did write me an apology letter a few nights after her initial reaction. I suppose after sleeping on her words and watching how different I was acting, she had the opportunity to reflect. I had come home one night and she was already asleep. I found a letter on my sink in my Mom's handwriting. It read:

> *Pyper, I am so sorry for how I reacted when you shared what happened to you. You caught me off guard and I regret how I handled the situation. I am always here for you if you want to talk. I'm truly sorry. I love you. - Mom*

## *Step 11*

### *Denial*

*I* wanted to start my senior year at college and try to forget about you. My mind had blocked the event and I suppressed it - hoping to never discuss or think about it or you again. But that wasn't the case. My mind, our friends, and my conscience couldn't and wouldn't let that happen. The little reminders, inside jokes, and pictures were still there.

I didn't know how to cope with all of it. After the response I got from my Mom, I didn't know where to go or who would believe me. Who would believe that it had nothing to do with drinking or what I was wearing?

I remember when I got back to campus I went to the counseling center to meet with Ken. Ken had become my counselor two years prior. I used to see him every other week in order to keep life in perspective and to have a healthy and safe place to talk, vent, laugh, or cry. I sat right down to catch him up on the summer. We talked about the goofy moments at the bars, dancing, work, and adjusting to being a senior team captain. I remember sliding in a one liner, "Oh yea, and I'm pretty sure I was raped, but I don't want to talk about it right now." And that was it.

When the meeting was coming to an end, he came back to the one topic I was trying to avoid, and simply asked me, "I know you don't want to talk about it right now, but are you doing okay?"

I said the only answer I knew to not be judged, "Yes."

## Step 12

## Sibling Trust

With Thanksgiving around the corner I was scared to go home for the Thanksgiving after the assault. I didn't want to go to the beach, and it would be the first time I would see my Mom since we had last spoken about the night with you. I wanted someone in my family to be there for me incase I got myself in a situation that I was uncomfortable with. I knew I couldn't tell my Dad for it would cause too much drama and I would be forced to explain more than I wanted. Therefore, that brought me to my Brother.

My Brother and I had become much closer since Dad's illnesses and I knew I could trust that he wouldn't overreact. However, I was still scared to have to share my story one more time and that now, my Brother too would know my new secret.

My Brother could tell over the phone that I was upset and was trying to tell him something. He remained patient as I organized my thoughts. He listened as I told him about what you did to me. He was sorry I had to go through something like that alone. I recall one of his first comments was, "I am so sorry to hear you are going through this, but I am always here for you." He went on to tell me that he had a teammate who just went through this entire experience herself. He reassured me that it was not my fault and that I needed to go back and speak with Ken and work through this with him.

Although I could hear the anger and hurt in his voice, he never once made it about him. He was sympathetic, patient, and listened to every word I said. Most importantly, he believed me. During Thanksgiving break, he never left my side. It was the first Thanksgiving that I can remember where I didn't come to the beach.

## Step 13

### The Phone Call

Do you remember the first conversation we had after time passed? It was over Christmas break, the December following the rape. I remember pacing upstairs in my room, through the hallway, into my Brother's room, and back into the hallway as we spoke for that hour. I cannot remember who called who or why we actually agreed to speak, but we did.

I recall trying to listen to your side and almost chuckling as your view of the night unfolded. You attacked my words the second I mentioned the word rape again. I told you I did not hate you, but I had no desire to ever see you, hear about you, or talk to you again. I remember you telling me, "I can tell you, this experience changed me, and I'm different now."

That last sentence haunts me to this day. For you to say that, proves that you know what you did was wrong and violent. However, for some reason, you cannot admit it. I remember getting off the phone and thinking, *Well, maybe I really did help you.* Yet time passed and I heard similar stories from Mark about you or about you hitting on his girlfriend. Sounds to me like nothing has changed. How do you even look another woman in the eyes? How do you hold a woman without recalling that night with me? Are you still aggressive? Pushy? Assertive? Do you know what "this isn't a good idea" means? Whenever I hear you have a new girlfriend, I just want to call her and tell her to get out while she can.

# Step 14

## Getting By

As the next few months passed I did my best to wrap myself up in soccer, friends, and enjoying the fact that I was a senior in college. What were you doing? Were you partying and repeating that night with someone new? My mind was consumed, and I wasn't ready to admit that you raped me. I drank every chance I could. I carried my hurt and anger on and off the field, and there were days I felt that I wasn't even there. I went through the motions and floated along. And it was my senior year! I should have been living up every minute, living the dream, but that just wasn't the case.

There were days I couldn't get out of bed. Days I didn't want to fake being okay. Days I wanted to avoid thinking that everyone who looked at me knew about that terrible night with you.

To top it off, I chose unhealthy and self-destructive ways to cope with my pain, confusion, and anger. I went out almost every night. I got drunk and slept around, trying each time to grasp my sense of control that you stole from me. There wasn't one person I felt safe with, comfortable with, trusted, enjoyed, or wanted to really be with. I was lost. Even though I was constantly concerned that if I put myself out there, that I would be raped again, I continued the search for control.

I recall, during many of the temporary fixes of sexual partners, that I would freeze up in the middle of the act, as flashbacks of you came rushing through my mind. If I didn't tell them to leave right away, I would often cry, shake, or just shut down, saying nothing at all. I completely closed down. However, unlike you, most of them respected me, listened to me, and several often just held me and let me cry. They didn't ask questions or make me talk; they simply just made sure that I was okay. Granted, I never got any callbacks. But like the alcohol, they were at the time, the only way I knew how to cope.

Since the rape, I cannot allow myself to be vulnerable or be in certain sexual positions. I have learned that I need to see a face or I will displace myself back to that infamous night. The desire and excitement of dating is hindered because of the fear of putting myself in a situation to be raped again. That night has impacted my life every day and I am still traumatized.

There are still times that I am at the beach with Mark and I'll spend the night at his house. For some reason we have remained in contact, even though each time we are together, I am reminded of the pain of what happened that night. He often suggests that I sleep in that same queen bedroom because that night doesn't cross his mind, like it does mine. I find myself reliving everything all over again as I ask to just sleep on the couch, in the other room, or even with him so that I don't have to spend another night in that queen bedroom. Mark will call me high maintenance as a joke, when there is nothing funny or entertaining about my request.

It took me until spring to discuss that night with Ken, and together we figured out more healthy ways to cope, and I wish I had gotten help sooner. After receiving help, there were still moments I questioned if I could have done something differently to stop you. But if I sat all day wondering about the "should haves" and the "could haves," I wouldn't have given my mind the necessary energy to heal. It has been a long process, but one where I have learned a lot about my family, my friends, and most importantly, myself.

I still wonder if you coped at all. Did you wonder or feel the same thoughts? Did you just go on and live up your senior year, your senior football season, your life? Were you able to enjoy it?

## *Step 15*

## *End of the Rope*

*I*t seemed that everywhere I turned, there were reminders of our friendship, that night, and the violence. It was spring of my senior year in college that we received our fourth (out of ultimately eight) e-mail of the year from the Vice President of Student Affairs that there was another sexual assault on campus. Eight, and I know now that those were only the reported ones. There is no doubt there were a lot more that went unreported. It was after the fourth e-mail that I couldn't take it anymore. It was all around me, and this time the e-mail was about one of my teammates. I decided it was time to take a stand against this act of violence.

I went back into Ken's office and unleashed the previous six months of pain. He had heard about my teammate and said, "I thought you might be coming in soon." I told him about the night at Mark's, how you didn't listen to me or believe me the next day. I talked about my Mom's reaction to my guilt, fear, insecurities, and distrust. I shared details about my coping and sleeping around to grasp the control you stole from me. I didn't hold anything back.

It was in Ken's office that I learned I would be all right and safe. I know now that I am just very aware and sensitive to the topic. I made the choice with Ken to engage and commit to healthier ways of coping. I began a journal, I became celibate, and more importantly, I managed my drinking.

After bumping up from going to see Ken from once every other week to once a week, he informed me that there was a sexual assault survivor group that was starting. He suggested it might be another healthy way to cope, and it would act as another sense of support as I went through the healing process. I was very skeptical at first. Would I know anyone in the group? Would they believe me? What would they think? Would I be welcomed into the group or would I be an outcast? Would they judge me? I began to wonder if you talked to anyone about that night.

I recall my first encounter with those incredible women. Women that would soon be called friends. They had only had a handful of meetings before I joined, and I didn't say anything the first time I went. I quietly sat in the circle and observed. I listened to stories, methods of coping, struggles, and concerns through laughs and through tears. It wasn't overwhelming, but more, a relief. I was no longer alone.

# Step 16

## Phoenix

*I*t wasn't until the second meeting with the survivor group that I felt comfortable enough to speak and open up. It didn't hurt that someone had brought Milky Way Bars to the meeting. It was over the next three months that the six of us began to grow as individuals and a group. Friendships were built as we shared stories, laughed, cried, and sat in silence together.

I recall sharing the anger I had toward you and toward Mark for still associating with you. I shared my disappointment in my Mom's reaction and how guilty I felt for sleeping around. I shared how I cried, how I felt completely disrespected and dirty as I failed to grasp control over my sex life. It wasn't until one girl looked at me, handed me a tissue, and said, "Pyper, I call those guys my 'coping boys.' They don't count. I had thirty-two of them." Then another said, "I had those too!" I was relieved to know that I wasn't alone.

I began looking forward to our meetings. As a group we would sometimes get dinner together, and we had a group e-mail chain to stay in touch. It was comforting and refreshing. One meeting instead of focusing on our experiences, we spent the hour determining a name for our group. We came up with *Phoenix;* it symbolized rebirth and a fresh start out of the flames of violence.

Occasionally, we would come into a meeting and there would be a new face. We would always welcome them with open arms and hope that we could help them as much as we had all helped one another. My teammate was one of the new faces and it was great to have her there, although I wish the circumstances were different. Sometimes I felt guilty that in my being there, I was taking away from her healing or focus. I didn't want her to hold back because I was there or sensor herself because of me. Likewise, selfishly, I didn't want to ever have to sensor myself. Luckily I never did, so I hope she didn't either.

Toward the end of my senior year there was a very violent rape off campus. Someone broke into an apartment and raped a student while making her roommate watch. Two weeks later she came to the *Phoenix* meeting.

I knew her, we had classes together, and she sat next to me in Biology. She didn't say anything the entire meeting and never came back. I saw her in class the next day and I said hello, hoping that if she wanted to talk she would know I'd be there for her. Sometimes I wonder if she stopped coming to meetings because she recognized some of us and felt ashamed. A few weeks later she wasn't in my class anymore. I still don't know if she left school all together to heal, or perhaps she didn't feel comfortable in my class because I could put a face to the rape. Regardless, I realized she was just at a different stage of her healing than I was. It took me more than two weeks to get help, it took me almost a year. I find myself thinking about her often, hoping she is finding her way and support.

Some meetings were harder than others, and some meetings felt a lot more productive than others. But either way, we all helped each other grow, cope, and heal. More importantly, it taught all of us that we weren't alone.

So I must ask you Jason, if you didn't rape me as you claim, why would I be here over five years later still healing? I didn't make this up. No one could make up this pain, the feelings, the confusion, and the betrayal.

*Step 17*

*Making a Difference*

$\mathcal{A}$s all of this was going on with me, what were you doing? Did you go to a group? Did you seek counseling? Did you continue with your aggressive ways? How many other girls in your life feel like I do? I have a feeling I'm not the only one.

I took all the anger, guilt, frustration, confusion, pain from you, and my teammate's assault, and put my energy into educating instead of drinking and "coping boys." I prepared myself to complete a Sexual Assault Awareness Program for the school. I researched facts, statistics, stories, pictures; contacted survivors and convicted sex offenders; and put together an educational evening dedicated to all of those who have been affected by sexual assault. My goals were similar to those of this letter - to raise awareness, educate, and perhaps prevent one person from being a survivor of or performing an act of sexual assault.

I had told Mark, Kristin, and Kevin about what I was doing. As I figured, I got the support I needed from Kristin and Kevin, whereas Mark was skeptical. He was trying to support me, but I could hear in his voice that he wanted this entire thing to go away. The funny thing was I even thought about inviting you. I thought maybe this would be the way to tell you everything I couldn't before. That you would finally understand my side of the story and realize the pain you caused me. However, I decided that the focus of the night was on education. I didn't want to be stressed about having another sex offender present. Now I often find myself wondering if you would have come. Would you have actually listened?

The research I found for the program was remarkable. Not only was it clear how uncomfortable the topic of sexual assault was for many, but I also once again discovered that I am far from being alone. Did you know that one in six women have survived sexual assault?[6] Actually, it is interesting how many people will talk about it, if you just listen.

After three months of gathering information, research, putting together slideshows, getting an a capella group to sing, and having sex offenders come and speak, I learned one month away that I did not have a place to host the event. I spoke to every administrator that I could. I was sent around the block and back, but I kept pursuing. People needed to hear what happened and people needed to know that sexual assault was real and all around us. My search for a venue led me to the office of the Vice President of Student Affairs. I explained the importance of the program, my goals, and my continued persistence. I will never forget how he sat and listened to me for forty-five minutes. He thanked me for my drive and supported my dream. He agreed that the program needed to be done. After explaining that my road block was that there were no available rooms or days to host the event, he looked at the main calendar for the college and studied it for about five minutes. He then took a pencil, erased one of his events and said, "I can do this somewhere else, take this room. What you are trying to do is more important." I would be lying if a few tears didn't fall at that moment. What an incredible man. I still have an e-mail that he sent me two years after I spoke. It read:

> Pyper, What a treat to hear from you. I remember well our first meeting. It was (and still is) clear to me that you were special and that what you were trying to do was terribly important. I was so right. Thanks for your message and best wishes.
>
> - Steve

It was people like Steve, my new friends in the *Phoenix*, and my roommate who once told me after I was thinking of giving up because I couldn't get a room to present my program, "Just do it for you, if you have to cancel it the night before, cancel it then, do not cancel it now and wonder for the rest of your life if you could have pulled this off."

Those final pushes of support motivated me to make a difference. Once all the survivors and convicted sex offenders were in order, I confirmed that an a capella group would perform.

I cannot even begin to describe to you what it was like to speak on the phone with people who were just as guilty as you. To dial the number of a convicted sex offender was incredibly intense, scary, and vulnerable. These men would now know my name, my phone number, and my school. They could find me if they wanted. I arranged with the school's counseling center to use their phone so it would track back to the school, and not to me. There were three men who were doing their service hours by giving back to the community. My program met those requirements.

Only one of the three convicted offenders showed up for the program. He had just been released from an eight-year sentence for rape and molestation of a child. When he arrived, I tried to be as professional as I could, and shook the man's hand. I showed him where the program would be and excused myself from the room. Once he entered the presentation room, I quickly went to wash my hands and gather my thoughts before having to go back in and speak with him.

I struggled to find a common conversation to pass the time before the program began. I focused on the schedule of events and when it would be his time to present. I asked him to speak about his crime, the results, and life in prison. Lastly, I requested that he concluded with what he had learned since the assault and if it had changed him.

I felt uncomfortable and unsafe. It reminded me of what it felt like to be in the same room as you. I called the other two offenders to see if they were coming, and for one of them, a woman answered. I remember my stomach dropping as I wondered if this woman knew the background of the man she was with. I imagine it would feel the same way if I called you and your girlfriend answered.

There was a slideshow that ran in the background that displayed graphic photographs and disturbing, but true, facts on sexual assault. The evening ran so smoothly. My teammates were incredible in helping to make it happen. I went from administrator to administrator until I got a yes. The word *no* was unacceptable. People had to learn or nothing would change. Eight rapes in one year plus me, and I promise there were more. And it wasn't just at my college. It happens at every university, school, office, and I guarantee everyone knows at least one person who has been assaulted. It just might not be known it if they haven't come out.

I became a sexual assault junkie. I could throw out statistics like it was my job. I even looked into doing public speaking on the topic, as a career, and applied to a handful of organizations. However, I decided at the time, it wasn't the right healing method for me. In 2006, one month before I graduated, I hosted my program. Over 250 colleagues attended again and there wasn't an open seat in the room. People sat mesmerized, frightened, and concerned that the girl they once knew as just a soccer player had a powerful story to share.

To this day, I have people come up to me or e-mail me thanking me for speaking and sharing my story. They inform me about how they had a sister, girlfriend, or father who was a survivor, and they will now have a better understanding of their experience. And then there were the survivors who reached out to me, having me be the first person they ever told. They knew they were assaulted and didn't know who to tell or who would believe them, but they finally could tell me. So in a sense, my program brought them peace, security, and trust; and I am forever thankful.

My fear, like writing you, was to be judged or not believed. However, after I spoke, I realized that was not the case. I have a text message still saved in my phone from one attendee: "Freakin awesome! I am so proud of you. I know I learned something, so it was a success." My three goals were met. I raised awareness, I educated, and I helped at least one person.

Have you helped anyone in the past five years? More importantly, have you helped yourself?

## Step 18

## Round Two

Two years later to the month, I was asked to return to my alma mater to speak during Sexual Assault Awareness Week for *Take Back the Night*. The fact that more people could benefit and be educated by my story was an honor. Plus, I had two more years of healing to share. *Take Back the Night* was an event I had attended once before with the *Phoenix* my senior year. It was a candle vigil, and I spent the evening listening to other survivor stories. Other male and female students spent hours sharing stories about their own experiences, friends and family, and how sexual assault had had a direct affect on their lives.

My plan when I went was to just go for me and to support my new friends in the *Phoenix*. I had no intention of speaking or sharing my experience. However, there was a silent moment, and I stood forward, and before

I knew it, I began to speak. I didn't share what happened between us, instead I said, "Thank you for everyone's love and support, I never imagined how powerful tonight would be, but this has been so inspiring, helpful, and healthy. Thank you for making me feel welcome." It felt right. I felt appreciative.

When I was invited back again, I felt the same thing. I was welcomed with open arms and spoke in front of over 150 students. This time, however, I didn't know anyone in the audience except for the woman who invited me to speak and the leader of the *Phoenix*. The soccer team was out of town for a spring game. They had a letter written in the school's colors waiting for me. I felt chills go down my spine, and I knew I could do it.

It was so refreshing and powerful to speak to an entirely new generation, demographic, and group of people. They weren't my friends; they were strangers who volunteered their time to hear my story. I had adapted the speech from two years prior and added more graphics, details, and information about my healing process. I'm not sure if it was the standing ovation, or the several students who approached me afterward to have private conversations, but it was amazing. I held back the tears as I knew I once again made a difference.

There were also other survivors that spoke and read personal journal entries and poems. It was the most amazing part of the night. The detail and power that came through those stories was amazing. The fact is that women are out there who share experiences like mine in their journals. How many more haven't told anyone? The graphic detail, and emotion that was going through their sentences was so admirable and sad all at the same time. Did you have any idea that I was doing all of this?

When the program ended, I stuck around in case anyone wanted to speak with me. A handful came up and said thank you. Some looked at me, some looked at the floor, and some simply walked out, perhaps not ready to face their own experience or maybe they just wanted to leave.

Then there was one male who was patiently waiting to speak with me. It took him a minute to gather his thoughts. I wasn't sure if I was about to be called a liar, or if he was just trying to sort through his thoughts in his mind to find the right words.

He said thank you. I once again had realigned; I reached my three goals. He went on to share with me his own experience with sexual assault. How he was molested by a male friend a few years prior. He told me how much he appreciated how graphic I was and how I was not ashamed to admit that I slept around. He said he coped in the same way that I did, and he thought he was alone until he heard me speak. I made a difference again, and it felt rewarding. A few days later, I turned my computer on and I had an e-mail waiting for me from Steve, it stated:

*Pyper, I was so very sorry I couldn't get over to see you and to hear you speak. Unfortunately I had committed sometime ago to an event at the same time. It would have been a treat to have seen you.*

*From what I have heard, the program was indeed a success. Having heard your first talk on the subject, I knew this one would be a home run and apparently it was. Thank you so much for doing this for us.*

*Best wishes for continued success to you. You richly deserve it.*
*- Steve*

## *Step 19*

## *The Reunion*

**D**o you even wonder where I was or why I wasn't around the summer following the rape? Did it cross your mind I wasn't around because of you? I went out West to escape you and the bullshit. I wanted to rediscover myself, become independent, and have fun. It wasn't healthy to be at the beach and around all of you. It had only been six months since I had seen you last. I wasn't ready. Would you have been?

At that point, the last time I saw you was the winter after it happened. I was at the bar with Kristin, Mark, Kevin, and another one of your past romances, Laura. I always wondered what happened between you and Laura because your friendship dissolved as quickly as ours. Did you do the same thing to her? To my knowledge, she doesn't know about what you did to me. Yet, I have a feeling if she did, a few stories about you two may come out as well . . .

You must have been at the bar with some friends from home. I saw you from afar and just wanted to leave. But, I didn't want to make a big deal out of it, and figured I would just keep my distance. I had my back turned to you and I was talking to Laura; you came up to us pretending nothing had happened, gave Laura a huge hug and kiss on the cheek, and then turned to me and did the same. I didn't see it coming, and my knees crumbled, and I felt like I just relived that entire night in about five seconds. I was frozen in fear and shock once again. I found myself quickly processing your touch and my body naturally shut down. When I had the strength, a few seconds later, I walked away and asked Kristin if we could go home.

I think about that night all the time. How different would it have been if I slapped you across the face or confronted you in front of all of our friends? Would our friends finally realize how big of an impact that night has had? Would they have finally admitted you are a rapist?

Based on their actions now and that they are still friends with you, I know now that they will always pick you. Like you, they don't want to admit this happened. I am slowly pulling away from Mark. Why would I want to be friends with someone who doesn't support me, respect me, believe me and remains best friends with a rapist? For whatever reason, I stay passive, not wanting to cause drama. However, this is real, Jason. Our friends should know who you really are and should stay away from you.

There is rarely a day that goes by that I don't think about that summer. Every time I am back at the beach, I fear running into you again.

It doesn't help that Mark rarely tells me if you are around. Each time I turn the corner to reach Mark's house, my heart starts pounding with anticipation that you are near. That is no way to live. The anxiety of coming to the beach is more cost than staying away and continuing to heal. And all of this could have been avoided, if you didn't rape me.

# *Step 20*

## *Choosing Sides*

*I* often wonder if my name is mentioned to you as much as yours is to me. Do you cringe too? Do you get quiet and reflect? Do you just want to tell whoever it is to shut up because you don't care? Why don't they get that I don't want to hear your name, or about your life, or your parents, or your sister *ever* again? I don't care! The only time your name needs to come up is if you're going to be in the same place as me, so I either don't go or have time to mentally prepare myself through different potential scenarios. I'm not ashamed or afraid in regard to you. I have accepted that night; I just prefer to not have to be on guard all night when you are around. Even though you are still controlling my actions at times, I am still proud at how far I have come in my healing and acceptance process.

There isn't a day I go down to the beach that running into you doesn't cross my mind, and it terrifies me. Every time I see a suburban, like the one you drove, my heart feels like it stops. But I guess our friends don't think it's a big deal, which breaks my heart.

It was like that one time in the early summer of 2008 when I saw you, and I had no clue I was going to. It was that weekend we went to lunch by Mark's boat. I was out with Kevin the night before, and he invited me to go on a boat ride, so I said I'd love to. He neglected to inform me that you would be joining as well. Not to mention how Mark offered for you to come on the same boat as me when there were two boats going. If we had been on the same boat, I don't think I would have made it through that day.

Do you remember the day? Did you know that I would be there? Did it shock you when I wouldn't even look at you, or that I left my sunglasses on so you couldn't see my tears? Did you notice how stiff and tense I was during lunch? What did you want to say? Because I didn't say a word to anyone, I just wanted it to be over.

Did it cross our friends' minds that your presence would bother me? Did it cross yours? I remember you looking at me and I left my sunglasses on, dodging your glare. I remember how your shade turned ghostly white when it struck you that you might actually have to speak with me. My anger toward Mark and Kevin for that moment has never really gone away. Perhaps anger isn't the right word. It is complete betrayal, hurt, and confusion. Just like our experience three summers prior.

I can recall docking the boats and waiting for you to walk ahead so I didn't have to wonder where you were. I wanted to be aware of your presence the entire time. I remember walking to the bar and seeing you order a drink, and look at me, like you actually were going to buy me a drink. I turned away pretending I didn't see and got my own. As our table was ready, and the eight of us went to sit down, I was stressing about how this was going to turn out.

Was it better to deal with sitting next to you if that was the only seat open, or across from you, so I had to stare at you the entire two hours? Did any of this even cross your mind, or was it just a normal lunch for you? I saw an open seat next to Kevin and sat down, asking one of the girls to take the other seat next to me before you reached the table. It wasn't until half way through lunch that I excused myself to go to the ladies room, where I cried, and had to get a grip to get through the rest of lunch. The mask I was putting on to protect you, and not cry in public, or pretend I gave a shit about what you were saying was eating away at me. Every time you spoke, I wanted to get up, hijack a boat, or hitchhike home.

When I returned, Kevin asked if I was okay. He was being his typical joking self, tapped my knee, and said, "You've been awfully quiet, buddy." At that moment, I pulled my sunglasses down, just enough for him to see the redness in my eyes, and it was like a light bulb went off. His face dropped in shame as he realized what this day must have been like for me. He said to me, "I'm so sorry, I didn't even think about it." I responded with, "It's all I ever think about."

Kevin never let go of my leg under the table for the rest of lunch. Why do they still associate with you? How do you even look them in the eye? It was about two weeks later when I saw you at our friend Hannah's graduation party. Once again no one told me you were going to be there. When I walked outside on the deck, I saw you and Mark playing Cornhole. You were between Laura and me, and she was waving to me and calling me over. As I gathered the courage to walk across your game, I felt like spotlights were glaring down at me, and your eyes were following my every move. I guess you got the point from the previous encounter because it was like we had never met. I wondered what the others were thinking. Five years ago, I would have run over to hug you and laugh with you.

In fact, we probably would have shown up together and been partners at Cornhole instead of you and Mark. I'm sure your story is different. The thing is if nothing happened that night, as you claim, then why am I still affected? Why am I so sensitive to the topic? No matter how you want to define that night it was wrong, and you never should have crossed that line.

I do not hate you. However, I have anger and pain toward you and our friends. Summers have changed. Things that we all used to do together are no longer.

## Step 21

### Acceptance

*I* don't know how much you keep up with my life through Mark. But, I have had two serious boyfriends since that summer. There were moments when I was with them that I would get quiet. They both understood, didn't pry, and would just hold me. It was because you were an ass and decided to completely disregard my feelings that it took me two years after I was raped to even *begin* trusting guys again. Today, I sometimes still cry. Yet there are a lot more days that I take a step back and say I've told my story, I've educated, and I'm making a difference.

Even while I was writing you this letter, there were times I just wanted to get away. Stirring all this back up was tough. There were months that went by that I couldn't even look at the letter. I was too familiar with the feelings that would come from reopening it. The rush of emotions, memories, and often sleepless nights were not always on the top of my priority list. Even though I had spoken twice at my alma mater, writing it was so different. I dug memories up that I had suppressed and hadn't thought about since that night.

Thanks to you, I am an educator now. I am blessed to have experienced this trauma because I know true trauma, pain, distrust, and most importantly, I know myself and that I will be okay. Will you listen now? Will you admit to this? Do you know this is about you?

When I look back on the past, I recall everything I just wrote you, but at the same time I recall a lot of good too. The healing process for me is still continuing. I have a feeling the thought of you will always be on my mind when I come to the beach or hear your name. But, I know that as I continue to heal and accept, I will continue to grow as a person.

This entire experience does not define who I am; rather, it is something that happened to me, between us. Through all of this, I have become stronger and more independent. I trust and rely on my healthy coping methods and support systems and try not to judge my healing by how much or little I cry. I take each day as it comes, and I am grateful each day for a few incredibly supportive friends, family, and personal growth. I truly believe that I can overcome anything, for I am stronger as a friend, daughter, and person. I will never doubt my inner voice again. I am actually strangely thankful for the wake up call.

I wish you the best of luck now and in the future. I hope one day you will learn to accept all of this, and perhaps realize this letter is actually written to you.

-   Pyper

# Epilogue

## Continuing to Heal

*I* am living proof that survivors can move forward and find happiness again. But every survivor's time frame will be different, for every survivor's situation is different. There are good people out there wanting safe and healthy relationships. Five years ago, I was not ready for safe and healthy. However, I have dated two great men who understood my past, appreciated me for who I am, helped me focus on the future, not the past, and never pushed me out of my comfort zone.

I did not write this letter to preach, change the past, or deface Jason. I wrote this to all survivors who are in different stages of their own healing. Know that you are not alone, and you can cope in healthy ways in order to get through the pain and confusion. It is possible, even if your struggles seem insurmountable.

I know I cannot change what happened, and I am not sure I will ever fully forgive Jason. However, I would be irresponsible to leave the impression that all survivors are women, and only men rape. I wrote this story because nights like the one that happened to me should never happen to anyone and if they do, tell someone. If your personal preference is to have the assault go unreported it is still important to talk to someone about what happened.

There are several national and local organizations that want to help survivors. In addition, there are various conduits to seek help and guidance including survivor panels, groups, and hotlines that can be reached twenty-four hours a day. (Several hotline numbers are listed on page 95). Confidentiality is not compromised through these help lines, so have no fear of losing anonymity.

Jason raped me, and I am a sexual assault survivor. In America, rape is one of the most unreported violent crimes, and my experience was one of the 60 percent of rapes that go unreported to the police.[6] People who rape or perform an act of sexual assault should be behind bars.

I hope after reading my story, the impact sexual assault can have on survivors is realized. These survivors could be anyone, including friends, family, or someday yourself.

I share my experience because I can relate to many survivors. I am Greek affiliated, I am an athlete, and I am social. I consider myself strong and never would have imagined something like this happening to me. I always imagined that I would kick a guy in the nuts or run fast enough away. Yet when I was being raped, that instinct never kicked in. Research shows that most rape victims do not scream in panic, despite common beliefs. Victims exhibit a spectrum of emotional responses to assault: calmness, hysteria, laughter, guilt, apathy, or shock.[3] Every individual is different with how they handle and cope with trauma. I personally was in shock that my best friend was not listening to my pleas and that he was trying to convince me that what he was doing was acceptable. I did not have time to think.

Afterward, it took me a long time to accept what had happened to me. My group of five was destroyed. Today, we get together without Jason, or they get together without me. They will still call and invite me when he is around, which almost hurts more, because it is as though they think time will pass and I will forget.

Time *will* heal things, but time will not let me forget. They think I overreacted; they just want it all to go away. However, the thing is, no one asks to be assaulted. No one wants to feel like shit, feel as though all control has been lost or have their body be unwelcomely groped. People cannot make up that feeling.

Sexual assault awareness does not end with being informed about the frequency and details of rape. There is an underlying desensitization to the subject in everyday life. How many times do you hear someone say, "We're going to get raped by this team" or "Oh, that exam just raped me?" Losing a game is not the same as being raped, and a piece of paper can never feel the emotions that a survivor will feel. A piece of paper will never know what it is like to be violated and have all sense of worth and value stolen from it. A piece of paper will never know the pain, confusion, and rebirth that a survivor will experience.

You can do your part. Catch yourself and catch others. Call people out when they make unnecessary comments about sexual assault. You never know the story of the person sitting next to you. Be considerate. Do not judge. Inform. More importantly, stand up for what you believe is right. I have done this on numerous occasions, and I never hesitate, because in calling someone out, I am helping to educate one more person on the topic of sexual assault.

The best advice I can give to friends and family of survivors is, it is natural to feel overwhelmed, scared, hurt, helpless, and emotional. Someone that you love and care deeply about is telling you something very personal because they trust you and want someone to listen. Try not to ask for details, doubt or question; because, every doubt or question will make your loved one feel that they are wrong to come to you or to anyone. And in reality, the details do not matter. Assault is assault, and that is the only thing that matters.

The important thing is for survivors to feel supported, to speak up, to report, and to educate. We *need* survivors and friends and family of survivors to speak up. Do not let abuse be a distasteful topic. Make it a reality. Own it. It is nothing to be ashamed. Be proud to speak up. Be proud to report. Be proud to educate.

To the individual directly impacted by sexual assault, you are not the person who was raped. You are a *survivor.* You have control of how the topic of sexual assault is perceived today and in the future. Do not let the topic of sexual assault continue to be a distasteful subject.

The signs were there. My head was telling me it was wrong, I had tears in my eyes, I had a knot in my stomach, and I was uncomfortable. I was trying to convince myself that I was fine when I was not.

Listen to that inner voice. There is never a reason for anyone to feel uncomfortable. Yes, it can be awkward to ask the person you are being intimate with if they are comfortable; however, that is certainly better than violating or raping that person.

For the past five years, I have worn a bracelet on my wrist from the *Phoenix.* All the women in the group purchased matching bracelets with a quote created from a member in the group engraved on the inside. The quote has been an important part of my healing and I am sure to many others in the group. I hope it can help any survivors reading this book.

*You may have touched my body, but you can never touch my soul.*

I realize that when I look back my life has not been bad. Yes, I have lost loved ones, pets, friends, and have been heartbroken, but in comparison, I would have to say that I have been relatively lucky. I have friends who have divorced parents, who have lost siblings, who battle cancer, who are suicidal, who grew up in violent homes, who have alcoholic parents, who face drug abuse, or who were neglected as children. I do not share my story in an effort to compare others' past experiences to mine. Everyone has importance in life. Everyone has topics that have deep value and meaning. Although the experiences may be different, we all feel similar emotions and feelings of love, fear, anger, depression, and happiness. The overall goal is to get to the stage of acceptance.

I know my future will have many more ups and downs. I cannot change the past or take back that night. However, that night or this letter does not define who I am. The past instead helps me to grow as a person, sister, daughter, and friend. I hope everyone can learn from the past and continue to grow.

Thank you for taking the time to read my letter.

God Bless,
Pyper

# Note to the Reader

*I* wanted to dedicate a section of the book to the several journal entries I wrote in regard to Jason, the rape, and my healing. I found a journal to be an extremely healthy and refreshing way to cope. There were nights that I could not sleep or times before I headed home for the holiday that I had to tell someone about my thoughts. That someone became my computer and my journal. These are some of my innermost thoughts, concerns, and struggles as I went through my healing process.

*January 1, 2006*

*I figured it was the first of a new year. I have wanted to keep a journal to keep my thoughts in check for years, and finally it's time. It has been a pretty crazy year. I graduate in a few months, and I made plans to go to out West after graduation, instead of the beach. Seeing Jason last month really threw me for a loop. I realize now that no matter what I do, he will still always be around. My only option is to not put myself in the situation to see him. Don't really want to be down at the beach - don't want to see Jason - and to be honest, tired of the same scene. Love that group, always will - but kind of over it.*

*February 15, 2006*

*Soccer is killing me. It's my senior season, and I should love every minute, but I am just not healthy. Maybe I should talk to Ken. I don't really feel like having another person judge me, not that he would, but this is just eating away at me.*

*March 2, 2006*

*Another rape on campus. This is getting ridiculous. I think this is number six. I make seven. I'm sure there are more of us. I went in to talk to the coaches today. They offered me a "free pass" that if I am just having an off day or mentally need a health day, I can take it. I feel like I'm taking the easy way out, but every one of these e-mails is a reminder of what happened last summer. I graduate in a few months and all I can think about is seeing him again. I should be focused on my senior year and my friends. However, whenever I am with my guy friends I feel on edge, and my girlfriends don't know.*

*April 20, 2006*

*Only a few more days to go until I present my Sexual Assault Awareness Program. I have had a lot of roadblocks. My roommate has been awesome in keeping me going. If it wasn't for her, I probably would have backed out already. I'm nervous about who will show up. Will people not believe me? Will people think I'm making it up? Will people think this isn't rape? What if there are* guys I have hooked up with or people that are supposed to be my friends in the audience who won't talk to me anymore? Ken says these people were never my friends in the first place if that is the case. The important thing is to focus on finishing it and realizing that if I reach one person, I will be successful. I was thinking of inviting Jason down. I told Mark I was doing this, and he just doesn't get it. It drives me up the wall. Maybe he'll get it when I'm not around this summer. Probably not.

August 2, 2006

Out West is awesome! I love being away. I met a guy, Jared. He's really been my first real relationship since Jason's encounter. I don't think it will go any further than a summer fling, but it has been a nice, slow adjustment back to reality. He is like no one I have ever dated before. He has tattoos, didn't go to college and smokes. I know he sounds bad, but I told him about Jason, and he respects me. I feel safe. He doesn't push me to do anything that I don't want to do. Mom wouldn't get it, but it's much deeper than what people see. For the first time in a year, I feel somewhat safe. And to be honest, right now, that feels pretty good.

January 16, 2007

It makes me a little nervous to be in a college city setting, nonetheless the fear of being raped again. Not knowing anyone, the area etc. Having to re-trust people and leaving it up to me with who knows my past. It's a little nerve racking. Been thinking a lot about Jason, and not about that night but more the fear of it happening again.

*February 20, 2007*

*I wonder what he is doing now. I hear he has some job on Wall Street. I got an e-mail from our mutual friend Amanda the other day, the one who was roommates with his ex-girlfriend in college. I wonder if she knows what happened. I wonder if he was that aggressive with his ex.*

*June 5, 2007*

*Well, this sucks. I'm single again. After everything that happened two years ago - why do I want to have to put myself back out there and have to explain myself all over again. But I don't really want to be alone either. I still feel like I don't know and need to date other people. But that's scary because then I have to go put myself back out there and feel unsafe again - but perhaps that's a good test for me to grow and regain my self confidence . . .*

*June 24, 2007*

*I do miss knowing I have someone to have sex with that is safe - and I have to admit when I was drunk I wanted that again. Maybe that's a little reminder that I shouldn't be drinking too much. Plus then if I don't have a one night stand I don't have to worry about being raped again . . . I really need to work on keeping that in check.*

*April 8, 2008*

*When I got to the room the lady who organized it handed me the card from my team they were away and couldn't make it - so that was awesome . . . They had musical performances and then in between they had readings from a new magazine on campus* which is all about sex. Anyone can write in, poetry or essays or words about sex. Anything they want. So for the aspect of the night, they pulled about 10-12 readings about sexual assault/rape. It was the most amazing part of the night. I spoke for about 25 minutes - I messed up a few times, but I think in the end I got my point across. I had changed my speech around from the first time I did it - and tried to pull in statistics from the college so it was relevant. I didn't know a soul in the audience except for two adults that I knew through campus and the woman I had just met who organized it. I suppose I touched some people because when I said "thank you" I got an immediate standing ovation! It was really rewarding.

*May 22, 2008*
I think I'm scared to see Jason this weekend if I run into him.

*August 1, 2008*
I usually really look forward to the summers so I can go to the beach, well to be honest that isn't the case anymore. I've seen Jason more this summer then I've seen him in two years and I just don't enjoy going there anymore.

*December 15, 2008*
Well I haven't written in a while, I guess that means I've been doing ok, or else just busy as hell. I'm writing a book. I feel good about it; it is keeping my mind busy.

*April 13, 2009*

*My boyfriend, Chad sometimes mentions his uncle, Jason. Every time he speaks about his love for his uncle, having never met the man, I automatically revert back to that night with Jason. I can't seem to escape that memory or his name. It is so hard because I don't want Chad to sensor himself around me, but at the same time I cringe each time.*

*August 27, 2009*

*The entire Jason thing and being at the beach has really taken its toll. It's amazing how being around here really acts me up - and I don't even realize it. Last night Chad kept asking me what was wrong, and I didn't know except I felt protected, concerned and just flat out "off" . . . As I started venting the true reason came out - Jason. Here I am back in the old stomping grounds and for some reason, Mark STILL doesn't get that I just don't want to hear his name. Tonight at dinner he was talking about becoming business partners with him. Are you serious?! What the fuck? Where the hell is your loyalty? Do you seriously still think nothing happened? I cringe at his name and the conversation about his ex-girlfriend - ugh what I would give to have her know what I think of him . . . I don't know what hurts more - the fact that Mark is still friends with him - or the fact that tonight Mark and Kristin disrespected me and talk about him like I give a shit. I don't want to hear his name EVER again! Ugh, it makes me sick. I was so close tonight to just telling both of them that I think I've been rather freakin' tolerant, but enough is enough. If you're going to be friends with him, which clearly you are, fine, but please out of respect for me, stop talking about him in front of me.*

It crushes me, sets me back and demoralizes me. I don't care if you don't understand or want to understand, but I want nothing to do with him or anything to do with him and his friends. Please stop.

March 27, 2010

Kristin called me tonight to catch up. She wanted to share her crazy shenanigans from St. Patty's day. She shared how she went out in the City and partied at, ready for this... Jason's house! I almost threw up in my mouth and hung up on her. But, for some reason instead, I pretended to care about the details of her night so I didn't upset HER! This is getting ridiculous. Now she is going to his house? What the fuck?! Am I worthless? Does our friendship mean nothing to her? Where is her loyalty? I somewhat understand Mark, but Kristin? Come on now!

June 8, 2010

I couldn't take it anymore. I finally confronted Kristin. She mentioned Jason last week in passing on the phone and I have just been, off since. They just don't understand that hearing his name automatically means that I am guaranteed to be "off" for at least two days. I felt bad, but I finally stood up for myself. I told her if she still expects to ever be in my wedding that she needs to pick me over Jason, always, no exceptions. I don't care if she is with Mark and Mark is with Jason, she needs to leave. She apologized and attempted to explain "her side." She said she had no idea I was so upset and she will stop talking to him etc. She admitted she was out *of line and that her loyalty should be to me and in the future it will be. So, next stop, Mark.*

December 5, 2010

*My book is almost finished! I cannot believe how far I have come in this process. It is incredible to look back on where I once was in my healing process, and be a few months away from publishing a book. It is incredible how time does help and heal the pain. Life has a way of working out and I am blessed to have the support of family and friends to complete this book and make additional progress in my healing. I know I have more to do, but I am a lot stronger now than I was five years ago or even one year ago. I am proud.*

# References

1. Bureau of Justice Statistics. *Rape and Sexual Assault: Reporting to Police and Medical Attention.* 1992-2000.

2. "Campus Attacks" FBI. *<http://www.d.umn.edu/cla/faculty/jhamlin/3925/myths.html>* (4 Dec. 2010).

3. "List of Rape Myths." *University of Minnesota. <http://www.d.umn.edu/cla/faculty/jhamlin/3925/myths.html>* (4 Dec. 2010).

4. National Center for Policy Analysis. *Crime and Punishment in America.* 1999.

5. "Rape Myths." *Illinois Coalition against Sexual Assault (ICASA). <http://www.icasa.org/docs/RapeMyths_fact_sheet.pdf>* (4 Dec. 2010).

6. "Reporting Rates." *RAINN. <http://www.rainn.org/get-information/statistics/reporting-rates>* (4 Dec. 2010).

7. U.S. Department of Justice. *2005 National Crime Victimization Study.* 2005.

8. "Who are the Victims?" *RAINN. <http://www.rainn.org/get-information/statistics/sexual-assault-victims>* (4 Dec. 2010).

# National Sexual Assault Hotline Information

**NDVH - National Domestic Violence Hotline**

1.800.799.SAFE (7233) or 1.866.331.9474

*www.ndvh.org*

**NSVRC - National Sexual Violence Resource Center**

1.877.739.3895

*www.nsvrc.org*

**RAINN - Rape, Abuse & Incest National Network**

1.800.656.HOPE (4673)

*www.rainn.org*